THE BIBLE TELLS ME SERIES

Selected stories from the Old Testament in five volumes showing God's love for the children of earth and the development of His plan to restore our sin-marred world to its original perfection.

Book 4

About God's People From Slavery to Sinai

By Gladys Sims Stump

Pacific Press Publishing Association
Mountain View, California
Oshawa, Ontario

Cover art by John Steel
Inside art by Joe Maniscalco
Design by Ichiro Nakashima

Copyright © 1982 by
Pacific Press Publishing Association
Printed in the United States of America
All Rights Reserved
ISBN 0-8163-0461-0

Preface

Bible stories have been rewritten and told over and over again. What child does not thrill to the stories of Creation, of Noah building an ark, of baby Moses, Daniel in the lions' den, baby Jesus, and a host of others? There have been many books written with these stories and others as their theme. Then why another series of Bible storybooks?

The stories in this series have been carefully selected to show in historical sequence the working out of God's plan for a perfect world. In other words, these books have the theme of redemption running through them like a golden cord—God's provision of grace, should His original plan be upset by rebellion. These books are not just a series of Bible stories. Each book brings the reader a little closer to that perfected plan when God will restore everything to the way it was at the beginning.

The author of the books in *The Bible Tells Me Series*,

Gladys Sims Stump, was laid to rest before her total concept was completed. Because of her love for children she desired to make even the very young understand God's love and care for them, and how His plan for complete restoration includes every person born in this world and involves, in fact, the whole universe.

The fresh, unique approach of this series will appeal particularly to the child of six to nine; but the contents, simply told, unfolding the story of God's love and care, will interest readers of every age. God's plan, though universal in scope, focuses on the individual. Christ would have died just for me, or for you! It was to portray this love that the author worked so earnestly on this set of books.

What a joy when God's plan finally reaches fulfillment and Gladys Sims Stump meets the many readers of her stories and hears the words "I learned about God's love through your books."

The Publishers

Dedicated

To boys and girls everywhere
and
to the memory of my parents,
William L. and Nettie Warren Sims,
from whom I first heard the
wonderful stories of the Bible

Contents

Satan's Plan or God's Plan? 9
God's Plan and a Basket 15
In the Palace School 27
Moses Makes a Choice 29
From Prince to Shepherd 37
Moses' Special Work Begins 40
Moses in the Palace Again 47
The Plagues of Egypt 55
The First Passover 63
The Children of Israel Leave Egypt 74
The Pillar of Cloud 79
At the Red Sea 85
The Journey Beyond the Red Sea 99
Food From Heaven 105
Water From the Rock 119
How God Destroyed the Amalekites 122
Moses' Family Joins Him 127
Sinai at Last 135

Satan's Plan or God's Plan?

God's plan never fails.

He often uses people to carry out His plan.

God had a person ready to build an ark so as to save the people who loved and trusted Him when He destroyed the world by a flood.

He had a person ready to save a whole nation from starving during a bad famine.

Joseph was the man God had ready to help the people in Egypt and also in Canaan when the famine came.

Joseph, the son of Jacob, had been sold as a slave and had been brought to Egypt.

God used him to save the people from starvation.

Joseph sent for his father, Jacob, to come to Egypt and live.

He also sent for his brothers and their wives and all their children.

These people were called the children of Israel.

Jacob's name had been changed to Israel many years before.

Now all these people, seventy in all, came to Egypt to live.

After the famine they stayed in the land.

They grew rich there.

They grew in number too.

God had promised Abraham and Isaac and Jacob that He would make of them a great nation.

But Abraham had died.

Isaac had died.

Jacob finally died in Egypt, and his descendants were foreigners living in Egypt.

They certainly had not become a great nation.

Then Joseph died.

The children of Israel still stayed in Egypt.

They were getting along very well.

Many, many years later, a pharaoh who did not know about what Joseph had done for the country came to the throne.

He saw that the children of Israel were rich and had some of the best land in Egypt.

There were hundreds and hundreds of these Israelites in the land.

This new pharaoh thought that someday the Israelites might take over the country.

Pharaoh decided to do something about it.

He made the children of Israel slaves.

God had told Abraham many years before that this would happen.

He also told Abraham that someday these people would leave Egypt and go back to the Land of Canaan.

They would become a great nation.

Many of the people who were slaves forgot about God and what He had said.

They forgot what their fathers and grandfathers and great-grandfathers had taught them.

Many of the people began to worship idols just as the Egyptian people did.

But there were always some who were true to God—the God who had created the world.

Those who were true to God were unhappy to see their children taking part in the Egyptian worship of idols.

Those who did not turn to idols and the Egyptian way of worship prayed to the God of heaven and asked Him to help them.

"Oh, dear God," they prayed "please take us out of this place.

"We remember your promise to Abraham, Isaac, and Jacob.

"We beg You to deliver us soon."

It was a sad, sad time.

The pharaoh set taskmasters over the slaves.

The taskmasters forced the slaves to work harder and faster.

They whipped the people and showed them no kindness.

Weeks, months, and years went by.

Even though the slaves, the children of Israel, had to work very hard, God blessed them.

He gave them great strength and helped them to keep well.

Their numbers grew and grew.

When Pharaoh saw this, he became angrier than ever.

Something would have to be done to stop these people from growing stronger in number.

Pharaoh decided on another plan.

"We will destroy every baby boy that is born to the children of Israel," he said.

But that didn't work.

No one wanted to destroy a newborn baby.

The women who helped the mothers when their babies were born did not carry out Pharaoh's plan.

But still Pharaoh was determined to get rid of the babies.

"If the baby boys grow up," he said, "they will fight against us."

At last Pharaoh and his advisers thought of a new plan.

Satan helped them think up this plan.

Satan knew that God had a plan to take the

children of Israel back to the Land of Canaan.

He knew the promise made to Abraham and to Isaac and to Jacob.

He would spoil God's plan if possible.

"If I can just get the baby destroyed who will lead God's people out of Egypt, God's plan will fail," Satan decided.

This was the plan, and Pharaoh put it into action.

All baby boys born to the children of Israel were to be thrown into the river Nile.

What a dreadful plan!

God's Plan and a Basket

Now Levi had been one of Joseph's brothers.
Both Joseph and Levi were sons of Jacob.
Jacob was a son of Isaac, and Isaac was the son of Abraham.
Now, one of the descendants of Abraham was a girl named Jochebed.
She was one of the family of Levi.
Jochebed was born in Egypt.
When she grew up, she married a man named Amram.
Amram was also related to Jacob.
He was a descendant of Jacob's son, Levi, too.
Jochebed and Amram were both slaves.
They knew what it was like to live the life of a slave.
But they both served God.

Jochebed and Amram had two children, a girl named Miriam and a little boy named Aaron.

When Aaron was three years old, God sent another baby into the home.

This baby, another boy, came after Pharaoh had made the law that all baby boys born to the children of Israel should be thrown into the river Nile.

"We mustn't let anyone know we have kept our baby," Jochebed said to Amram and to Miriam and little Aaron.

"If the soldiers of Pharaoh hear about him, they will come and take him from us.

"We will hide our baby.

"We will not let him cry.

"We just can't have anything happen to this precious baby.

"Do you understand?"

Miriam promised, "I won't tell anyone, and Aaron is too little to tell anyone."

Little Aaron stood by shaking his head.

Then Amram spoke up: "It's almost time for us to be freed from slavery.

"I've been counting the time.

"You know, Abraham was told how long we would be in Egypt.

"God promised we would be delivered from Egyptian slavery."

"Perhaps," Jochebed said, "our baby will grow up to help.

"I believe God's promises.

"This baby may be the one who will help God carry out His plan."

For several months they hid the baby at home.

They all did their best to keep the baby from crying.

They kept their secret from everyone, and the Egyptians didn't know there was a baby in the house of Jochebed and Amram.

One, two, three months went by.

The baby had been growing.

It was hard to keep him hidden away.

It was hard to keep a three-month-old baby quiet.

"What shall we do?" Jochebed asked one day.

"If our baby is found, he will be thrown in the river; and we will be in trouble for having hid him so long.

"What can we do?"

They prayed about it and asked God to help them keep their baby.

One day Jochebed had an idea.

She told it to Amram.

She told him that she would make a little basket of reeds.

Tall reeds grew by the water's edge, and these she would use to make a basket.

She would use pitch to smear on the reeds so

that water would not seep into the basket.

Then she would place the baby in the basket and the basket in the river.

"Our baby will be safe because we will place the basket boat among the tall reeds by the water's edge.

"God will look after him," Mother Jochebed said.

Miriam, the baby's sister, helped Mother Jochebed fix the basket.

They put soft blankets in the basket and then placed the baby in it.

Mother Jochebed carried the basket down to the river's edge.

Miriam followed her mother.

She knew that God would protect the baby.

Mother Jochebed had told her God had a special work for this baby to do.

When they got to the river, Mother put the basket in the water among the tall reeds.

"I will hurry back to my work," Mother said.

"Please stay close by and watch."

Jochebed went back to her work.

Miriam stayed and watched the basket boat and prayed.

She found a place among the tall reeds where she could see the little basket boat in the water.

Both Miriam and her mother must have prayed that God would take care of the baby in the little basket boat among the reeds.

Everything was quiet.

The little basket boat rocked up and down in the water among the reeds.

After a while Miriam heard voices.

From her hiding place among the reeds she looked out to see who was coming.

She saw some people coming to the river.

Then Miriam saw some maidens coming to the river.

They were laughing and happy.

All of a sudden Miriam saw someone with the maidens that she had seen before—it was the princess.

The princess was the daughter of Pharaoh, the ruler of the land.

The princess and her maidens were coming to the river to bathe.

Miriam watched breathlessly as they came closer to the water.

The princess saw the basket boat.

She ordered one of her maids to get the basket boat for her.

When the maiden brought the basket to her, the princess looked inside and saw the baby there.

"This must be the baby of one of the children of Israel," the princess said.

"Some mother has done this to save her baby.

"I will keep this baby and bring him up as my own son."

Miriam, who had not been far away, hurried over to the princess and asked if she would like to have someone nurse the baby for her.

"Yes, go find someone to care for the child for me," the princess said.

Miriam knew just who she would get.
Of course, the woman Miriam ran to get was no other than Jochebed, the baby's own mother.
Jochebed didn't need to be urged to hurry to the bank of the river.
There she saw her precious baby in the arms of the princess of Egypt.
She did not tell the princess that she was the baby's mother.
But when Miriam told the princess that this woman would be glad to care for the baby, the princess put the little one in Jochebed's arms.
How happy Jochebed must have been!

"Take this baby to your home.
"Take care of him for me.
"I will pay you wages for your work.
"I will keep him as my own son.
"I am going to call him Moses because I took him out of the water.
"That is what Moses means."

Miriam and her mother lovingly carried the little basket and the baby back to their home.

Now they would not have to fear that the baby would be taken from them.

This baby would be safe because the princess, the daughter of Pharaoh, said he would be her own son.

Jochebed would be the baby's nurse.

Jochebed and Amram would have the baby, who had been named Moses, in their home for several years.

"I will teach him about the true God," Jochebed said.

"I will teach him about God's promises to Abraham, Isaac, and Jacob.

"Perhaps God saved him to help deliver us from this terrible slavery.

"Yes, perhaps he is the one."

Little Moses grew fast as most babies do.

He learned to walk and to talk.

He learned to pray.

He learned about God, the Creator.

He learned about Adam and Eve in the Garden of Eden and of their wrong-doing.

Moses learned all about God's plan and how Satan had tried to do away with God's plan.

He learned that Satan is always trying to get people to do wrong things and join in rebellion against God.

Jochebed and Amram told Moses about Abraham, who had been chosen to be the father of a great nation that was always to worship the true God.

They told him about the promise God had made to Abraham, Isaac, and Jacob; and they explained to him how it was that the children of Israel were in Egypt and how they had become slaves.

It didn't take Moses long to learn that the slaves were despised by the Egyptian people.

No doubt Jochebed often told Moses that he would have a special work to do for God because he had been saved from Pharaoh's cruel decree.

The years that Moses lived with his real mother

and father and his sister, Miriam, and brother, Aaron, passed by quickly.

When he reached his twelfth birthday, he had to go live in the palace.

No doubt during the twelve years he lived with his real parents, the princess must have visited him often.

She may have taken him out for rides in her chariot.

She may have taken him to the palace from time to time to show him off to her friends.

But when he was twelve, she took him away from the little home where he had been living and took him to the palace.

The palace would now be Moses' home.

He learned now that someday he might be pharaoh of Egypt.

He would be trained in all the duties of a ruler of such a great country.

In the Palace School

Moses started to school in the palace.
He was taught many things.
He learned to read and write.
The Egyptians tried to teach Moses the worship of their gods.
The Egyptians worshiped many different gods.
They worshiped the sun, moon, and stars.
They worshiped the Nile River.
They thought that cows were sacred.
They even thought cats were sacred too.
In the palace were images of what they thought their gods looked like.
Moses was shown these images.
The priests tried to get Moses to bow down and worship the images.
But Moses refused.

"How foolish!" thought Moses.
"I will not worship such things.
"There is only one true God.
"He is the Creator of all.
"You worship the sun, the moon, and the stars.
"I worship the One who made the sun, moon, stars, and all things.
"You worship the river.
"I worship the One who made the river.
"You worship cows and other animals.
"I worship the One who made the animals."

"You can never be a pharaoh unless you worship our gods," said the priests.

But Moses still refused.
He was always polite to his teachers, but they couldn't get him to believe in their gods.
Because the pharaoh expected Moses to be the ruler of Egypt some day, he must learn many things.
One of the things he must learn was how to lead the armies of Egypt in battle.
Moses became very wise, and he learned to be a good general.
This made the Egyptians honor him.
The Bible says that Moses knew all the wisdom of the Egyptians.
Moses was wise in words and deeds.

Moses Makes a Choice

Satan had worked to make God's plans for the children of Israel fail.

He thought that if he could get all the boy babies killed he would make the plan fail.

He wanted to destroy the one that God had planned to use to lead the Israelites out of Egypt.

But God had overruled the terrible decree of the pharaoh.

Yes, God used this decree for good.

By this decree God worked it out for Moses to grow up in the palace.

Moses would become well educated and learned.

Moses would be trained to be a leader.

God was getting him ready to do a great work for Him.

Even though Moses lived in the palace and called the princess "Mother," he never forgot who he was.

He remembered that he was the son of Amram and Jochebed.

He did not try to hide this.

He was not ashamed of his people, the children of Israel.

He always remembered that his God was the God of the children of Israel.

He often visited with his people.

He saw how hard it was to be slaves of the pharaoh.

Moses talked with the people and tried to get them to have hope and trust in God.

He tried to get them to believe that God would deliver them someday.

As Moses watched his people at work, often he felt very, very sad.

He wanted to help in some way.

Then one day angels told Moses that God planned for him to deliver the people from slavery.

Angels also visited the leaders of the children of Israel and told them that the time was near when God would deliver them.

The leaders were also told that Moses was the one to lead them out of slavery.

By now Moses, a great, skillful general, was nearly forty years old.

He had shown his skill in leading the army of the Egyptians to victory in battle.

Moses thought about how the angels had told him that he was the one to deliver the children of Israel.

Moses thought that this meant he would do this by leading them in battle.

"I can lead my people in a battle against the Egyptians," he thought.

"I will no longer be called the son of Pharaoh's daughter.

"I will give up all the glories of the palace.

"I will instead join my people, who worship the true God," vowed Moses.

"The pleasures of a sinful life last only a short time—then they are gone," he thought.

"But in the service of God the blessings are everlasting."

Moses knew all about the palace which was his home, and he thought about how it would be to be a pharaoh and the ruler of Egypt.

But he was willing to give it all up.

He would rather take his place with God's people.

He was sure that someday those who served God would have more than just a king's crown—more than a king's palace.

He was sure that God would really reward those who chose to serve Him.

So Moses made his great promise to God and himself.

One day Moses was out in the part of the land where the children of Israel worked.

He saw a poor Israelite being beaten by an Egyptian taskmaster.

Moses made up his mind to do something about it.

"I might as well begin my work for my people," he thought.

Quickly Moses killed the Egyptian.

Then Moses looked all around to see if anyone had seen what he had done.

No one was near except the Israelite he had helped.

Quickly Moses buried the Egyptian in the sand.

He thought that this was the way to deliver Israel.

The next day Moses saw two Israelites fighting. He spoke to them about it.

"Who made you a prince to rule over us?" asked the one who was in the wrong.

"Do you intend to kill me as you killed the Egyptian?"

Then Moses knew that what he had done was known.

No one had seen Moses kill the Egyptian except the Israelite whom Moses had defended.

The Israelite must have talked too much about it to someone.

Soon the story would spread.
Soon all the Egyptians would know about it.
Soon Pharaoh would hear about it.

When Pharaoh did hear about it, he said, "Does this mean Moses intends to lead his people against the Egyptians?

"While Moses lives, our government will not be safe."

When Moses heard that Pharaoh was angry with him, he decided to run away.
He decided to go a long way away from Egypt.
Even though Moses had done wrong, God still loved him and He directed his steps.
God would overrule this rash act of Moses to work out what God had long planned for the children of Israel.
No doubt, as Moses walked along, he thought about the sad mistake he had made.
Moses had taken things into his own hands.
God had promised to deliver the children of Israel with the help of Moses.
But it was not God's will to deliver them by warfare.
Moses had misunderstood.
Moses was not yet ready for his great work.
He had still to learn the same lesson of faith as his fathers had learned.
Abraham, Isaac, and Jacob had to learn not to depend on man's strength or wisdom.

His forefathers had learned that by God's power and in His time His promises came to pass.

And there were other lessons to be learned too.

Moses needed to learn patience.

He needed to learn perfect trust and obedience.

He would have to unlearn many things that he had learned in Pharaoh's palace.

From Prince to Shepherd

At last Moses came to the land of Midian, where the Midianites lived.

Tired and lonely, he sat down by a well to rest.

By and by he saw some shepherd girls coming toward the well.

He counted seven girls coming with their sheep.

He watched as they started to draw water for their sheep.

Soon other shepherds came with their sheep.

They tried to drive the girls away.

Moses stood up and ordered those unkind, selfish shepherds to allow the shepherd girls to come back to the well.

Moses then helped the girls water the rest of their sheep.

When the girls returned home, their father asked, "Why are you home so soon?

"Oh," they answered, "a kind Egyptian helped us."
"He drove those hateful shepherds away.
"Then he helped us water our sheep.
"He was very kind."

Then Jethro, who was the girls' father, asked, "Where is the man?
"Why didn't you invite him home with you?
"Go and call the man and invite him to come and eat with us."

It turned out that Jethro made Moses feel at home at his place, and the two men learned that they were really related to each other.
After Sarah's death Abraham had married a woman named Keturah.
Midian was one of the sons of Abraham and Keturah.
So you see the Lord directed the steps of Moses to the home of one of his relatives.
Jethro, was a descendant of Midian, a son of Abraham.
Jethro served the same God as Moses did.
He was a priest in the land of Midian.
From this story we know that some of the descendants of Midian worshiped the true God, the God of Abraham, Isaac, and Jacob.

Moses stayed with Jethro and became a shepherd.

He became the keeper of Jethro's sheep.

After a time Moses married one of Jethro's daughters, a shepherd girl named Zipporah, a kind and loving person.

And Moses worked with Jethro's sheep for forty years.

As Moses led the flocks of sheep into the mountain country, he had lots of time to think.

He learned to love the beautiful hills around him.

He no longer missed the gorgeous palace and temples of the Egyptians.

"They can't compare with these beautiful hills and the things that my God can make," he thought.

He was glad to be away from the life of the palace and Egypt.

He was happy to be away from the priests of Egypt and their false gods.

Moses' Special Work Begins

As the years went by and Moses stayed in Midian as a shepherd, he often thought about his people back in Egypt.

He knew they were still slaves.

He remembered God's promises to Abraham and to Isaac and to Jacob.

Every night and every morning Moses prayed for his people.

While Moses lived in Midian and watched his father-in-law's sheep, the Holy Spirit helped him to write about the creation of the world.

Moses wrote the story of the beginning of things and about the days before and after the Flood.

He wrote the story of Abraham and of Isaac and of Jacob.

He wrote about Joseph and about the children of Israel, Jacob's sons and their families going to Egypt.

Those stories are in the first book of the Bible, Genesis.

Moses wrote that book.

He wrote other books of the Bible too.

But Moses knew that God had a special work for him to do.

He knew that it was almost time for the children of Israel to leave Egypt and go to Canaan, the land God had promised would be theirs.

How was it all going to happen?

One day while Moses was out watching the sheep near a mountain called Mount Horeb, he saw a strange sight.

He saw a bush on fire, and the bush kept burning and burning but didn't burn up.

Moses decided to go a little closer to the bush and see what was going on.

Suddenly he heard a voice speaking to him.

"Take off your shoes, Moses, for the ground that you are standing on is holy ground," the voice said.

"I am the God of your father, the God of Abraham, the God of Isaac, and the God of Jacob," the voice went on to say.

"I have seen the trouble of My people in Egypt, and it is time to bring them out of the land of Egypt.

"They have been slaves in that land for a long time.

"It is time to bring them back to the Land of Canaan.

"Now," the voice went on, "I will send you to Pharaoh, and you will bring the children of Israel out of Egypt.

Moses trembled.
He knew that voice.
He knew it was the voice of God.

"Who am I, Lord, that I should go to Pharaoh and bring the children of Israel out of Egypt?"

That same voice from the midst of the still-burning bush said, "Certainly I will be with you."
God talked to Moses for some time, telling him what he should do when he returned to Egypt.
Moses had a lot of excuses why he felt he couldn't go back to Egypt.

"They won't believe me," he said.

"What is that in your hand?" God then asked.

"Just a rod," Moses answered.

"Throw it on the ground," God said.

Moses dropped his rod, and it became a snake. Moses ran away from the snake, but God told

43

him to stoop down and pick the snake up by the tail.

He did as God commanded, and the snake became his rod again.

"Do this before my people so they will believe that the Lord God has appeared to you and sent you to Egypt," the Lord said.

Then the Lord told Moses to put his hand inside his cloak.

Moses did as the Lord had commanded.

When he took his hand out and looked at it, he saw that he had leprosy, a much-dreaded disease.

Then the Lord told him to put his hand back inside his cloak.

Moses obeyed; and when he took his hand out again, the leprosy was gone.

"If they won't believe after seeing these two signs," the Lord said, "then show them another.

"Take some water from the river in your jug and pour it out on the ground, and the water will become blood."

Even after having been given these signs Moses did not want to go back to Egypt to do as the Lord had asked him to do.

"I am not a good speaker," Moses argued.
"I—I stutter."

But God had even planned for that excuse.

"Is not Aaron your brother?"
"I know he can speak well, and he is coming to meet you.
"You will speak to him and tell him what to say.
"I will be with your mouth, and with his mouth, and will teach you what to say."

So Moses decided to go.
Moses' family, his father-in-law Jethro, his wife, and two sons went part way with him.
At last they had to say good-bye and return to Midian.
Moses went on alone to Egypt.
Just as the Lord had said, Aaron, his brother, met him.
Moses told Aaron all that the Lord had told him.
In Egypt they gathered all the elders of the children of Israel together and told them what the Lord had said and showed them the signs that the Lord had told Moses to show them.
The elders saw the rod become a serpent.
They saw Moses' hand turn white with leprosy.
They saw the water turn to blood when he poured it on the ground.
The elders believed their words.
They bowed their heads and worshiped.
It was almost time, according to the prophecy, that God's people should leave Egypt.

And just as God always does, He was going to keep His promise.

The elders told the people about what they had heard from Moses and Aaron.

How the news of what God was going to do for His people spread!

The word went from house to house among the children of Israel who lived in the land of Goshen.

But there were some who said, "I don't want to leave Egypt.

"I would rather stay."

"You are to go with us to the pharaoh," Moses told the elders.

Moses in the Palace Again

Moses and Aaron, with the elders, went to Pharaoh.

Up the palace steps the two brothers and the elders went.

It was the same palace that Moses had known so well as a young man.

The brothers, with the elders, were shown into the room where the pharaoh sat on his throne.

Then they gave the message from the God of Israel to the pharaoh.

This is the message that the pharaoh heard:

"The Lord God of Israel says, 'Let My people go that they may hold a feast to Me in the wilderness.

'The children of Israel are as a son to Me.

'They are even as a firstborn son.

'And I say to you, Pharaoh, let My son go that he may serve Me.

'If you refuse to let him go, I will slay your son, even your firstborn.' "

In disgust the pharaoh answered, "Who is the Lord that I should obey His voice to let Israel go?

"I don't know the Lord; neither will I let Israel go."

And Moses and Aaron said, "The God of the children of Israel met with us.

"Let us go, we beg of you, three days' journey into the desert to sacrifice."

But, no, the pharaoh had no intention of letting the children of Israel go.

Even before Moses and Aaron and the elders had gone to the pharaoh, he had heard of the excitement among the slaves.

The slaves wanted to rest on the Sabbath.

The pharaoh was angry.

"Why," he asked Moses and Aaron and the elders, "do you hinder the people in their work?

"Look, there are many of these slaves.

"We need their work, and you make them rest from their work."

Without another word Moses, Aaron, and the elders left the palace.

The children of Israel had in some ways forgotten what they had known about God's law and the Sabbath.

The taskmasters had made it seem that it was impossible to keep the Sabbath.

But Moses had shown the people that obedience to God comes first.

God had made His promises of freedom on the condition that the people would obey Him.

Moses had called attention to the Sabbath.

He had talked to the people about it, and Pharaoh had heard about it.

The people wanted to rest on the Sabbath.

Pharaoh feared that the Israelites were getting ready to rebel.

So he determined to make things even harder for them.

The Israelites had the work of making sun-dried bricks.

These were used to make the beautiful buildings that the Egyptians were building.

The walls were made of these bricks.

They were then faced with stone.

The bricks were made of clay held together with straw.

Now the pharaoh ordered that the children of Israel would have to furnish their own straw.

And they would be compelled to make as many bricks as usual.

If they had to search for something to use to make the bricks, they couldn't make as many.

They just couldn't do it!

The Egyptians had placed some of the Israelites to oversee the work of the people.

When the people didn't get enough bricks made, the Israelite overseers got in trouble.

They were cruelly beaten by the Egyptian taskmasters.

The Israelite overseers went to the pharaoh about it.

They thought that the blame was to be placed on the taskmasters.

But they soon found out that it was the pharaoh himself who was to blame.

Pharaoh answered them with a sneer.

"You are idle! You are idle!

"You say that you want to do sacrifice to your God."

He ordered them back to their work.

"It is Moses and Aaron who have brought this great trouble upon us," wailed the children of Israel when they learned that they would be forced to work even harder.

"It was better before Moses came and started trying to get our freedom," they said.

"It has only made matters worse."

Poor Moses!
He went to the Lord.

"Oh, why have You sent me?" he cried.

"Ever since the day that I went before Pharaoh, he has made more trouble for my people.

"And You haven't delivered them at all."

God answered, "Now you will see what I will do to Pharaoh.

"With a strong hand he will let them go.

"With a strong hand he will drive them out.

"Remember the covenant that I made with the fathers," said God.

The people had expected to be delivered without any trouble.

They had little faith and were not willing to wait for God's own time and way.

Moses told the people that God was really going to take them out of slavery.

But first God was going to show such great miracles that all the Egyptians would know that God is the only true God.

The children of Israel needed to learn some things about God too.

They were not ready to be delivered.

"Now go to the pharaoh again," God commanded Moses.

"Tell the pharaoh to let my people go."

"If Israel won't listen, how will the pharaoh listen to me?" answered Moses.

"Take Aaron with you and go again and demand that the pharaoh send the Israelites out of the land," God told Moses.

"The pharaoh will not do this until I have sent troubles upon Egypt," God said.

God wanted to show the pharaoh and the people of Egypt His great power.

God meant to show them how really feeble were their gods.

God meant to show the people that their mighty ones lacked true wisdom.

They had boasted of blessings received from their senseless gods.

God would hush their boasting.

Yes, God would glorify His name among the nations who would hear of His power.

God would by all these mighty acts lead His people to turn to Him in pure worship.

Again Moses and Aaron went to the palace.

They asked the mighty ruler of the most powerful kingdom to let God's people go.

The pharaoh demanded a miracle.

Moses and Aaron knew just what to do when the king demanded this.

God had prepared them.

Aaron threw his rod down before the pharaoh.

It became a serpent.

The pharaoh ordered his wise men to come to the palace.

In came the wise men.

"See what this man did with his rod," said the pharaoh.

And they all looked at the serpent there in front of the pharaoh.

Then the wise men threw down their rods.

To everyone the rods appeared to turn into serpents.

But now something really exciting happened.

Aaron's serpent went first to one, then to another, until it had swallowed up all the wise men's serpents.

Aaron's serpent didn't miss a one.

And now where were the wise men's rods?

The magicians had not really caused their rods to become serpents.

But by magic, helped by Satan, they had made it appear so.

Satan did not have power to change rods to living serpents.

Satan does not have power to make living things.

Only God has this power.

The Plagues of Egypt

It was Pharaoh's custom to go down to the river Nile every morning to worship the river god.

The next morning after Aaron and Moses had been at his court, they met Pharaoh at the river.

God had told Moses just what to do.

Once more Moses and Aaron told Pharaoh that God had commanded that the children of Israel be set free so they could worship Him.

But Pharaoh said No.

This time Moses told Aaron to lift the rod that he carried and hold it over the water of the river and then hit the water with the rod.

It was the Lord who told Moses what to do.

Moses told Aaron what the Lord had said, and Aaron did as Moses told him to do.

Suddenly the water of the river turned to blood.

The fish in the river died.

The people couldn't drink the water because it had turned to blood.

The smell of the river became foul.

Throughout the land of Egypt the water all had turned to blood.

Even when the Egyptians dug new wells for water, the water in those wells was blood.

For seven days all the water the Egyptians had or could get had been turned to blood.

But the children of Israel had fresh water for themselves in the land of Goshen.

God looked after His people.

Again Moses and Aaron went to Pharaoh and asked him to let the children of Israel go so they could worship God.

But again he refused to let them go.

Once more Moses told Aaron to stretch forth the rod over the river.

Frogs came up out of the river and out of the ponds and out of the streams.

Frogs! Frogs! Frogs!

There were frogs everywhere and in everything.

The Egyptians worshiped the river.

It had turned to blood.

They worshiped frogs too.

Now that the land was overrun with frogs, they wanted to get rid of them.

Because they thought the frogs were sacred, the people would not destroy them.

The frogs were in the cooking pots.

Frogs were in the beds.

Frogs were everywhere.

Frogs were all over the palace.

Frogs! Frogs! Frogs!

The Egyptian magicians and sorcerers could not get rid of the frogs.

At last Pharaoh called for Moses and Aaron and begged them to ask the Lord to take way the frogs.

He promised he would let the people go so they could worship their God.

Moses and Aaron asked Pharaoh to set a time when they should ask God to cause the plague of frogs to end.

When the time came and Moses prayed, the frogs died and the Egyptians had to gather them up and bury them.

Then Pharaoh hardened his heart again.

He would not let the children of Israel go.

Once more Aaron stretched forth his hand with the rod in it.

This time he stretched out his rod over the land.

And this time there were lice—lice everywhere.

The magicians and the sorcerers could not make the lice appear.

They told the king that this was God's doing.

The lice were on both people and animals.

How they all itched!

After the plague of lice came flies.

Swarms of flies—biting flies.

Although the Egyptians had been troubled by the water turning to blood, the frogs, the lice, and the flies, the children of Israel were not troubled by any of these things.

God protected His people.

Pharaoh now suggested that the plagues be stopped.

He would let the children of Israel worship and sacrifice to their God right there in the land of Egypt, he said.

But Moses said No.

Then Pharaoh said the children of Israel could take a three-day journey into the wilderness area and sacrifice and worship there if only the flies would leave.

The flies left, but Pharaoh at once changed his mind.

He would not let the children of Israel go.

Then all the animals of Egypt got sick with a deadly disease.

The animals got so sick they died.

But the animals of the children of Israel were spared.

God protected them from the disease.

Now Moses was told to take some ashes and sprinkle them toward heaven in the sight of Pharaoh.

As the fine ashes were scattered about in the air, wherever they touched people or animals, boils broke out.

Not only did a boil make a person look bad, it made him or her feel miserable too.

People and animals were covered with the terrible sores.

After the plague of boils came a storm — lightning, thunder, and hail.

This time, before the plague came, God gave a warning to all the people in Egypt that a terrible storm would come.

Huge hailstones would fall and would hurt and kill the animals if they were hit by them.

The people were warned to have their animals and themselves inside their barns or houses so that the huge hailstones would not hurt them.

Some of the Egyptians believed, and they stayed indoors and kept their animals in the barn.

But others did not believe.

The hailstones killed many animals and people and destroyed the fields and gardens.

But there was no storm at all where the children of Israel lived in the land of Goshen.

Some of Pharaoh's counselors said to him, "Let the men of the children of Israel go, and stop these plagues."

"Please ask God to stop the rain and hail and thunder," Pharaoh begged Moses and Aaron.

"I have sinned.
"I will let all the men go and worship God."

But Moses said, "No, we will all go."

Seven terrible plagues had fallen on the land of Egypt.

Now grasshoppers, or locusts, swarmed over the land.

Everything the storm hadn't destroyed the locusts did.

The locusts came in swarms like clouds that even blotted out the light from the sun.

Then darkness came over the land of Egypt.

For three days no one could do anything, because it was so dark.

But all the children of Israel had light in their homes.

Once more Pharaoh said he would let the people go if the plague was stopped; but when it was, he hardened his heart again.

Nine plagues had fallen on the Egyptians.

During each plague Pharaoh thought of letting the people go; but when the plague ended, he decided not to.

He hardened his heart, the Bible says.

The First Passover

The last plague was soon to fall upon the Egyptians.

Moses told Pharaoh that if he hardened his heart and would not let the children of Israel go, a plague would fall on Egypt that would cost the lives of all the firstborn.

God didn't want to bring this plague upon Egypt.

If only the pharaoh and his people had repented after the loss of their crops and cattle, the firstborn would not have had to be destroyed.

Pharaoh had forbidden Moses ever to appear in the palace again.

But God had ordered Moses to give His last warning, and Moses followed God's orders.

Yes, he went up those palace steps again.

He stood before the pharaoh and warned him of the death of the firstborn.

Pharaoh heard the words: "Some night soon at midnight all the firstborn of men and beast shall die."

Then, after giving the warning, Moses returned to the land of Goshen to give instructions from the Lord to the children of Israel.

"Now," said Moses, "we have almost come to the very time that God told Abraham about.

"We are going to get ready to leave Egypt.

"God is going to take us out of this land.

"We are going to be free."

This word went from house to house.

The elders saw to it that all the children of Israel heard the exciting news.

"You have heard of the last plague that is to fall upon the Egyptians," Moses said.

"You have heard what is going to happen at midnight on the night we are to leave Egypt.

"Now God sends me with these special directions to you, His people.

"Each family alone or with another family is to take a lamb, a perfect one, from its flock.

"Nothing is to be wrong with the lamb in any way.

"Bring the lamb to your house.

"You are to kill the lamb.

"The lamb represents the Promised One.

"You know that the Promised One someday will give His life for you.

"With a bunch of hyssop dipped in the lamb's blood you are to sprinkle the blood on both of the doorposts of your house.

"You will also sprinkle the blood on the lintel or top of the doorway.

"At midnight a destroying angel will pass through the land, and when he sees the blood on your doorposts and on the lintel, He will pass by.

"The destroying angel will not destroy the firstborn when he sees the blood.

"But if the blood is not on the doorposts, the oldest child will die.

"No matter how old the firstborn person in that house is, he will be slain if the blood is not there."

Some mothers and fathers had been the firstborn of their families.

These were in danger too.

"Be very sure," cautioned Moses, "that you do everything as God has commanded."

"And be very sure that all of your family is in your house with you.

"This is important.

"If one of you is in an Egyptian home, he will not be protected.

"You will not be protected unless you are in a home where blood has been put on the doorposts and the top piece of the doorway.

"After you have sprinkled the blood of the lamb, you are to roast its meat.

"You will then eat the meat along with unleavened bread and some bitter herbs."

As Moses told the Israelites about how to celebrate this first Passover Feast, he also told them that this was to be a special yearly celebration from then on.

This would help them always to remember how God had delivered them from the Egyptians.

As they killed the lamb for the Passover Feast, they were to think of the Promised One who was to come and die for their sins.

God didn't want them to forget.

"Tonight you will have to eat in a hurry, standing up, with your staff in your hand, dressed and ready to go," God said to Moses.

"We must be ready to leave on a moment's notice," Moses told the people.

"The Egyptians will chase us out; so be ready.

"This means that you must be packed.

"Have ready all the things you want to take, for we shall have to leave in a hurry.

"Each of you must go to the Egyptians before this night comes and ask for gifts of gold, silver, and other precious things.

"They will give these things to you gladly.

"This is part of the wages you should have had for all your years of slave work."

So the instructions that Moses gave were passed along to all the children of Israel.

They were going to be free!

On the evening of that day the Israelites killed the lamb and sprinkled the blood as God had commanded.

In so doing they showed their faith in God's protecting and saving power and in the Promised One to come.

There was much to do.

All the people collected the precious things that they were to get from the Egyptians.

The oxen were brought up; and the carts and covered wagons were loaded with the tents, bedding, cooking dishes, and other things the children of Israel wanted to take with them when they left Egypt and slavery.

The great flocks and herds were gathered together.

Everything was done swiftly, thoroughly.

This must have been hard to do when everyone was so excited.

It must have been a very busy and exciting time for everyone.

Moses, who had been the great Egyptian general, knew just how to divide all those people into companies with leaders.

How well God had led and trained Moses for his great work!

God had overruled in Moses' education in the palace of the pharaoh.

He knew that His great leader would need to know how to order His people's exit from Egypt.

Moses showed that he still knew how to do the work of a general even after forty years as a shepherd in Midian.

And the people were willing to follow the plans of Moses in their order of march from Egypt.

The people obeyed the command of God and followed His orders about the sprinkling of the blood and the supper they were to eat that special night.

Some of the Egyptians who had learned to honor the God of the Israelites begged to come into the shelter of an Israelite home on that night.

And the Israelites made them welcome.

At midnight they began to eat the special Passover supper.

All at once they heard screaming, shrieking, and wailing coming from the homes of the Egyptians!

Yes, the destroying angel had entered every home where there was no blood sprinkled on the doorposts.

It was dreadful!

But not one person in the families among the Israelites was harmed—not one.

All the Israelites had seen to it that the blood had been sprinkled on the doorposts.

The pharaoh, the priests, the servants, the people, all found their firstborn dead.

Then the pharaoh sent for Moses in the night.

"Go," he said; "go quickly.

"Take your wives and children, your herds and flocks.

"Go sacrifice to your God and ask your God to bless me."

And the people of Egypt cried out, "Go, or we will all be dead."

They showered the Israelites with gifts.

"Get out of our land," they begged.

Moses now gave orders for the people to start moving.

Quickly mothers and big sisters snatched up the bread dough they hadn't had time to bake.

They put the dough in the bread bowls and carried them on their shoulders.

The fathers and the big brothers were busy looking after the flocks and herds.

It was a real job to keep all the animals moving in the right direction.

Imagine how hard the fathers and their sons must have worked to keep all those herds and flocks in line!

And can't you hear the dogs barking?

You know how excited dogs can become.

"Hurry, hurry, hurry," was the word that was heard everywhere in Goshen.

But with all the little children and old people

and young animals, how could they hurry very fast?

They couldn't, though everyone seemed to say, "Let's hurry."

They surely had to get away before Pharaoh changed his mind again.

The hundreds and hundreds of Israelites were all leaving Egypt as God had promised.

Almost everyone was walking.

Perhaps a few were riding donkeys.

There were six hundred thousand men alone.

This was not counting the wives and children.

And all this great company was making its exit from Egypt in perfect order.

God had helped Moses to see to that!

The Children of Israel Leave Egypt

God's people left at the very time that God had told them of so long before.

Some of the Egyptians who had come to believe in the true God wanted to go along with them.

These Egyptians promised to serve and honor the true God.

They were made welcome.

Besides these, there were some who thought they wanted to go along and see the excitement.

These, with some of the children of Israel who had married Egyptians, went along and were known as the mixed multitude.

There was something else very important that the people took along with them.

Joseph had asked the children of Israel to promise to take his bones with them when they left

Egypt, as God had promised they would.

Moses and Aaron saw to it that the coffin holding Joseph's bones was brought out of its tomb.

It was loaded on a cart or wagon and taken along when the children of Israel left.

Yes, God had kept His promise to Abraham.

The children of Israel were free at last.

Before morning the Israelites started away from Egypt.

The Egyptians had really hurried them away.

"Go! Go before all of us are dead," begged the Egyptians.

"What can we do to help you get going on your way to sacrifice to your God?"

It was a good thing that each family had packed its things the day before so that the companies of people with their leaders were ready when the signal for departure came.

All wanted to hurry away from Egypt as fast as possible.

Not one Israelite man, woman, or child would be left behind.

They took their herds and flocks too.

When Jacob's sons had gone to Egypt, they had taken their flocks and herds with them.

During the time of the famine they did not sell their cattle to the pharaoh as the Egyptians did.

During all the time they were in Egypt the size of their herds and flocks had increased until at the time of their departure they had "very much cattle" and other animals.

Now they started out in the darkness of the night.

By the time the morning came, they were away from the land of Goshen.

No longer could they see the tall pyramids or the cities that they had helped build for the Egyptians.

But they couldn't travel very fast.

The caravan didn't cover many miles that first day.

It got only as far as Succoth.

Moses gave the order to make camp.

As the sun went down, all were glad to stop for the night.

Even the herds and flocks were glad to bed down, for they were tired too.

Everyone, we may be sure, was glad to lie down on a blanket or mat and go to sleep.

How good it must have been to sleep out there under the stars.

The day had been long.

The night before had been so exciting it is likely that no one had slept.

How good it was to sleep now.

Morning came too soon.

The people awoke to the sound of the trumpets.

"Get ready to go on our journey," the leaders called.

The people obeyed the orders from their leaders.

All wanted to put as much distance between the Egyptians and themselves as they could.

They felt that they should make as much time as possible.

They didn't want anything to keep them from getting to the Promised Land.

So as soon as they could get ready, they started again.

As they walked, they encouraged each other by talking and thinking about their freedom.

The Pillar of Cloud

On the second day's march suddenly there appeared something strange in front of the long line.

Whatever could it be?

It looked like a cloud.

Yet it was different.

It seemed to be in the shape of a tall pillar.

There was a brightness to the cloud.

It was a soft brightness something like the clouds in a sunset.

But it was diffrent.

What could it be?

When evening came, everyone stopped, ready to make camp.

All were glad when they heard the command to stop for the night.

The people had traveled from Succoth to Etham in one day.

This was a pretty good march for such a large caravan.

Here at Etham they made camp again.

Etham was on the edge of the wilderness, or desert.

Often in the desert or wilderness it gets chilly when the sun goes down.

But that cloudlike pillar seemed to provide warmth.

As the people made camp—pitching their tents, cooking their suppers, and caring for the animals—they watched the cloud.

They saw that the cloud had changed to a very bright light, as if it were on fire.

The whole camp was lighted by the cloud.

Moses explained to the people that God was in the cloud.

"When we look at the cloud," explained Moses, "we know that God is taking care of us.

"God is the leader of this caravan.

"He will protect and show us which way to go.

"In the daytime He will lead us by the cloud.

"We will follow the cloud.

"And as you have seen, the cloud will become a pillar of fire after dark.

"The pillar of cloud by day and the pillar of fire at night will always be with us on our journey to the Promised Land."

In their travels across the desert the cloud would protect them from the hot sun.

At night the cloud would give them light and warmth.

At Etham the people made more preparations for their journey across the desert.

One of the things that the mothers did was to bake the bread dough that they had brought with them from Egypt.

They would need this bread on their journey.

When all was ready, the companies took their places with their leaders and waited for the signal to start again.

Then everyone looked at the cloud.

The cloud started to move toward the south.

"Something is wrong," the leaders said.

"The cloud is leading us the wrong way.

"That isn't the way to Canaan.

"We are going toward the Red Sea.

"We should turn toward the northeast."

But Moses simply pointed to the cloud and said, "God is our Leader, you know.

"We must follow where He leads."

Moses may have explained why the cloud was leading them toward the south.

God knew the children of Israel had to be protected from the fighting Philistines, who would have attacked these slaves leaving Egypt.

The Israelites didn't know how to fight a war.

They didn't have enough weapons either.

They had only a few small swords, and they probably didn't know how to use them.

They had been slaves for many years.

Besides this, the Israelites really didn't know God very well yet.

God wanted a chance to teach them about Himself.

The poor Israelites during the time of their slavery had almost forgotten about God.

Had they known Him better, they would not have been frightened by the fighting men of the Philistines.

But God knew that this great company of slaves was not yet ready to meet such an enemy.

So this is the reason why God in the cloud led the people southward instead of through the land of the Philistines.

He didn't want the people to become discouraged.

What a wonderful and loving God He is!

The cloud went forward, and the people followed.

Already some of them were beginning to wonder about where their journey would lead.

Across the dreary desert they journeyed.

The children were tired.

The old folk were tired.

Everyone was tired.

They were all becoming weary of their journey.

But the wonderful cloud gave them shade as they trudged through the desert.

The wonderful cloud kept moving forward, and the people followed.

Then God revealed to Moses that Pharaoh would come after them but that God would deliver them from the pharaoh and his host.

At the Red Sea

The multitude of people came at last to the Red Sea.

The Lord now directed Moses to command the people to make camp beside the Red Sea.

They were in a rocky valley with high mountains on both sides of the valley.

Here the Israelites made camp.

They felt a little worried for fear they couldn't get away if the Egyptians should come—and some worried a lot about that.

Of course the cloud was there though, and this was a comfort to them.

The cloud stood still over the camp.

Meanwhile back in Egypt the pharaoh and his people began thinking about what had happened.

We can be sure that the pharaoh himself or one of his men had gone down to Goshen and looked over that part of the land.

The land of Goshen was really deserted.

The houses were emtpy.

There wasn't a single animal left, unless it was a cat or two.

If the Israelites left cats, they knew that the Egyptians would take care of them; for the Egyptians worshiped cats.

The whole place was deserted.

When the pharaoh and the others in the palace heard of the conditions in Goshen, they began to wish that they had never let the slaves go.

"Why they have taken everything they had!

"They don't plan to return, we can be sure," they said to each other.

"I was foolish to let them go.

"I was afraid to refuse them because of all those plagues," said the pharaoh.

And as the priests and others talked with the pharaoh, they all agreed that the plagues just happened, that they weren't caused by the God of the Israelites.

"Oh, why did we let them go?"

"Well, we are going after them.

"One of our tower guards sent me the news that

the Israelites are lost in the wilderness.

"They seem to have made their way in the wrong direction.

"The tower guard at Migdol says that they have camped by the Red Sea after wandering around in the wilderness.

"The Red Sea is only 80 miles from Egypt.

"We are going after them and will bring them all back.

"Everyone has heard that we are afraid of the Israelites' God.

"Nations around have been laughing at us.

"They have heard about those awful plagues.

"They have heard that the great nation of Egypt let its slaves walk away.

"We are all in disgrace.

"But we will bring those slaves back."

Then Pharaoh decided to get together the whole army and go after the children of Israel.

As fast as they could, the Egyptians got the chariots ready—all 600 of them.

Since the pharaoh was going along, his bodyguard went too.

In each chariot was the driver and a man who knew how to use his sword, spear, and bow and arrow.

Not only did the army and all those chariots get on their way, but even the priests went.

By taking the priests the Egyptians thought that their gods would help them.

So away they went at top speed.

"We'll bring them back!" they shouted as they raced over the desert.

When the Israelites were still far away, the Egyptians spied them camped there by the Red Sea.

Suddenly some of the Israelites caught sight of the flashing armor and the moving chariots of the great Egyptian army.

"They are coming after us," cried the children of Israel.

"What shall we do?

"The mountains are around us, and the sea is in front of us.

"How can we escape?"

Terror filled their hearts.

Some cried to God, but most of them blamed Moses for bringing them into such a place.

"Why have you brought us here, Moses?

"Have you brought us here to die in this wilderness?" they wailed.

Moses was very troubled that the people had so little faith in God.

God had already shown them great wonders.

How could they charge Moses with the dangers, when he had been following God's command?

It was true that they were in great danger unless God worked for them.

But Moses was not afraid.
He spoke to the people.

"Don't be afraid; just stand still and see what God is going to do for you.

"Today you will see how God will save you.

"The Egyptians that you see today you will see again no more.

"The Lord is going to fight for you.

"You must not complain.

"Have faith in your God."

The poor Israelites were so frightened that it was hard for the leaders to keep order.

"Can we be sure," some questioned, "that the pillar of cloud is really God leading us?

"Maybe that cloud is a sign that something dreadful will happen to us."

The Israelites had listened to Moses, but they couldn't believe they could be saved without doing something themselves.

It was really frightening to think that the Egyptians were coming upon them.

And then something wonderful happened.

Suddenly the people saw the great cloud lift and pass over the camp.

It came down—down between them and the armies of Egypt.

On the side next to the Israelites it was light.

But the cloud made a great darkness on the side between the Israelite camp and the army of Pharaoh.

It was like a thick, black fog on the Egyptians.

The chariot drivers had to call their horses to a halt.

The whole host of the pharaoh stopped.

So the Egyptians made camp.

In the camp of the Israelites the pillar of fire shone bright.

The Israelites were not so frightened now.

They began to have faith that their God would deliver them.

Moses had been praying for their deliverance.

Then God said to Moses, "Command the children of Israel to go forward.

"Lift up your rod and stretch out your hand over the sea.

"The sea will be divided; it will open and make a path for the people right through the sea."

Moses did as God commanded.

The leaders called to the people to get their families and animals together.

Then they were to go forward and march through the sea.

Moses lifted his rod.

He stretched it over the sea, and a wonderful thing happened.

The waters separated.

The waters made a wall on each side of a path—a path right through the Red Sea.

The Israelites walked through on the dry path between the walls of water.

The road through the sea was lighted from one side of the sea to the other.

Of course the animals didn't understand about it all, but they followed or were driven by their owners on this crossing in the sea.

At last they were all across on the other side of the sea.

It had taken most of the night for the huge multitude of people and animals to make the crossing.

In the morning light the cloud that had

separated the Egyptians from the children of Israel lifted, and the Egyptians saw what had happened.

The Egyptians were angry that the Israelites, who had been almost in their power, had found a way to escape.

Remember that it was still rather dark for the Egyptians.

But they knew that the Israelites were escaping.

They could see that the Israelites were far ahead of them on the road through the sea.

"Shall we follow them?" they asked each other.
"If they can go across that way, so can we."

The Egyptians hurried to get started.
The Lord looked at the host of Egyptians.

He saw the host that was with the pharaoh.

The Lord saw them through the pillar of cloud and the pillar of fire.

The Lord saw them start to cross on the same path that the Israelites had used.

He allowed the Egyptians to go into the sea path.

But suddenly the chariot drivers began to have trouble.

The wheels of their chariots began to come off.

The Egyptians became confused and frightened.

"The God of the Israelites is fighting for the Israelites," said the Egyptians.

They had dared to venture in the path that God had prepared for His people.

Now the Egyptians remembered about the plagues.

Now they began to fear that the God of the Israelites might deliver them, the Egyptians, into the hands of the Israelites.

"What shall we do?" they asked each other.

"We had better turn around."

But this was easier said than done.

In trying to turn around, how those 600 chariots became tangled up with each other!

God was fighting for His people.

He waited until the last Israelite was on the other side of the sea—and until all the Egyptians were in the sea.

Then God told Moses to stretch out his rod again.

At once the waters of the sea rushed together.

The Egyptians tried to save themselves, but it was impossible.

The Egyptians had failed to make the true God their god.

God had done everything in His power to bring this nation to accept Him.

But God will not force Himself on anyone.

Each person and nation must choose to serve Him.

Each one may choose rightdoing and live or may choose wrongdoing and die.

The Egyptians had chosen wrongdoing.

The sea covered them all, and not one escaped.

As the Israelites stood upon the opposite shore of the sea, they looked and saw in the morning light that all their Egyptian enemies were gone.

Then the people thanked the Lord for His wonderful care.

They were so thankful that they wanted to sing a song of praise to Him.

Moses composed a wonderful song of praise.

It is called the song of Moses.

Here are the words:

> "I will sing unto the Lord, for he hath triumphed gloriously:
> the horse and his rider hath he thrown into the sea.
> The Lord is my strength and song,

And he is become my salvation:
He is my God, and I will prepare him an
 habitation;
my father's God, and I will exalt him.
The Lord is a man of war:
the Lord is his name.
Pharaoh's chariots and his host hath he cast
 into the sea:
his chosen captains also are drowned in the
 Red sea.
The depths have covered them:
they sank into the bottom as a stone.
Thy right hand, O Lord, is become glorious
 in power:
thy right hand, O Lord, hath dashed in pieces
 the enemy. . . .
Who is like unto thee, O Lord, among the gods?
who is like thee, glorious in holiness,
fearful in praises, doing wonders? . . .
Thou in thy mercy hast led forth the people
 which thou hast redeemed:
thou hast guided them in thy strength unto
 thy holy habitation.
The people shall hear and be afraid. . . .
Fear and dread shall fall upon them:
by the greatness of thine arm they shall be still
 as a stone;
till thy people pass over, O Lord,
till thy people pass over, which thou hast
 purchased.
Thou shalt bring them in, and plant them in

> the mountain of thine inheritance,
> the place, O Lord, which thou hast made for thee to dwell in."
>
> —Exodus 15:1-17.

The great company of people sang the song of Moses.

The mountains echoed and reechoed the wonderful strains of the song called the song of Moses.

The Bible tells us that when the redeemed of the earth all gather before God's throne, they are going to sing the same song of Moses.

They will also sing a new song—the song of the Lamb.

The song of the Lamb is the song of man's redemption.

Each one of us can be there and join in the singing.

The Bible says that there will be such a great number of people there that no one can count them.

The Journey Beyond the Red Sea

The cloud moved ahead, and the children of Israel followed.

They traveled through a most desolate country.

The mountains were bare, and the plains were deserts.

It must have been difficult for the animals to find enough food.

Yet the Israelites were thankful and happy as they thought about God's wonderful care.

They were happy to be on their way to the Promised Land.

Toward evening the cloud stopped moving.

It was time for the Israelites to rest.

They pitched their tents and made camp.

And they were glad.

The day had been long.

Early the next morning all the people prepared to continue the journey.

On they traveled across desert country.

The sun shone down hot upon the people and their flocks and herds.

All day long they had watched for springs or wells of water.

They found none.

For three days as they journeyed they could find no water.

By the third day the water bags that they had brought with them full of water were empty.

Moses watched the cloud.

He knew this country well because he had looked after sheep here for many years.

He saw that the cloud was leading them in the

direction of some springs of water he knew about.

But he also knew that the water in those springs was bitter.

He was afraid of what the people would do and say when they discovered the water was unfit for use.

Moses didn't have long to wait.

He heard the joyful cry of "Water, water" when the spring was discovered.

As many as could crowded around the spring.

Every one was excited about finding this pool of water.

The first one who took a drink made an awful face and spit the water out of his mouth.

"It's so bitter we can't drink it."

The people began to complain and blame Moses for their trouble.

Many blamed Moses, but some remembered how God had led them.

Moses felt sad, but he knew God was the one leading them.

So Moses prayed.

He always asked God for direction and help.

God answered him.

The Lord God told Moses to cut down a certain tree and put it in the water.

So Moses gave orders to cut down a tree and put it in the water and then drink.

The water became sweet and good after the tree was put in.

There was enough water for all the thirsty people and all the thirsty animals.

And, of course, all the water bags were filled.

The people gave the place of the bitter water the name of Marah.

The word "marah" means bitterness.

Yes, God had first tested the people to see if they would trust Him.

Then He made the water sweet to prove how much He loved them.

It was a lesson to show them that God always has a way out of every difficulty.

It was after this happened that God made them a wonderful promise.

"If you will always listen to My voice, do what is right, listen to My commandments, keep My laws, then I promise to keep you from having any of the diseases which you have seen in Egypt.

"For I am the Lord who heals you."

When the people went to bed that night and looked up at the beautiful bright cloud, they must have thought about the promise that had just been made to them.

They must have thought about the conditions of the promise.

They surely knew by now that God would keep His promise if they did their part.

They were learning to have faith in God!

From Marah the people journeyed on to a place called Elim.

Here they were happy to find twelve wells of water and seventy palm trees.

Moses said, "We will make camp here.

"The cloud has stopped."

The nearby valleys provided pasture for all the animals.

The people camped at Elim for a little while before they continued on their way.

"We will never complain again," they must have said over and over while they made their camp at Elim.

And they meant it.

But Satan and his wicked angels wanted to

destroy the people's faith in God.

They hoped to destroy these people whom God had chosen as His special people, a people whom God had chosen to give to the world the story of the true God.

This is the reason, of course, that Satan and his host were determined to win them to their side or destroy them.

Let us think of this as we read the story of how God led His people to the Promised Land.

Food From Heaven

The Israelites had been away from Egypt just one month.

They were now encamped in the Wilderness of Sin.

Mount Horeb and Mount Sinai were two names for the same mountain.

Each day the Israelites traveled, they got closer to Mount Sinai.

Everyone was happy.

God was with them.

But one day the people noticed that their supply of food was running out.

The plants in the wilderness didn't promise to provide much food either.

And their flocks were becoming smaller and smaller.

How was food to be supplied in the future?

This was the question in the minds of the people.

The people began to worry about this.

"It's plain to be seen that we may starve out here in the wilderness," the people said to each other.

The people all seemed to forget that God would provide for them.

Finally even the rulers and elders joined in complaining against Moses and Aaron.

They seemed to blame them for what they were afraid would happen in the future.

Had anyone in that great company been hungry since the journey to the Promised Land had started?

But the people were afraid of what might happen in the future.

They imagined that their children would be starving after a while.

It seemed impossible that such a great number of people could be supplied with food in their travels.

This would be impossible without God's help.

God was trying to teach His people to depend upon Him.

At first only a few had started complaining about the food problems.

But others followed these few until it seemed the whole camp couldn't say a good thing about what might happen.

The people seemed to have forgotten the vow they had made never to complain again.

The people seemed to have forgotten what had happened during the plagues.

They seemed to have forgotten how they had walked through the sea.

They seemed to have forgotten about the water at Marah.

Satan had really worked to upset these people.

He was trying to turn them against God.

He and his wicked angels were delighted when they heard the complaining.

"We will win; we will win if we can make all of them distrust God," Satan said.

Finally the whole congregation joined in blaming Moses and Aaron for the danger they imagined they were in.

"We wish we had died in Egypt," they said.

"We wish that the Lord had killed us there along with the Egyptians.

"When we were in Egypt, we had plenty of food.

"We had meat, bread, fish, and vegetables.

"We had all the food there that we could eat.

"Here, you have brought us out to this wilderness to kill us with hunger."

On and on these angry people raved at Moses and Aaron.

"We want food!

"We must have food!" they shouted.

Poor Moses and Aaron!

But as Moses always did, he called on the Lord.

The Lord told Moses that He would send the people bread from heaven in the morning.

He said he would keep sending it until they reached the Promised Land.

"I will see whether they will keep My law or not," the Lord said.

The Lord gave Moses exact instructions regarding what was to be done with the bread that He would send.

"God tells me that He will provide for your needs," said Moses.

"This evening you will know that the Lord has brought you out of Egypt.

"In the morning you will see the glory of the Lord, even though you have murmured.

"Your murmuring has really been against God and not against us.

"But God will show you that He is not holding it against you.

"You know that He has sent us help every time we needed it."

Then Aaron spoke to the people and told them to look at the brightness shining in the pillar of cloud.

As he spoke, the people looked toward the cloud.

Suddenly the cloud shone with great brightness.

The glory and brightness of the Lord shone out in the sight of all the people.

The Lord Himself was in the cloud.

And again the Lord spoke to Moses and said, "I have heard all the murmurings of the children of Israel.

"Speak to them and tell them that this evening they shall have flesh to eat.

"And in the morning they shall be filled with bread.

"Then they will know that I am the Lord."

So Moses told the people what God had said about the food that He would send.

Toward evening the people noticed that the sky seemed to be getting very dark in one place.

Then suddenly, as the dark cloud came closer, they noticed it was a cloud of birds.

Closer and closer the birds flew.

Over the whole camp they came and lighted on the ground.

"It's quail! It's quail," the people shouted.
"Let's catch them."

And catch them they did.

Every family caught as many as it wanted.

That night the people had all the roast quail they could eat.

Some people made themselves sick, they ate so much.

But that was not all God was going to give them.

The best was yet to come!

In the morning the people got up early.

Sure enough, the ground was covered with something they had never seen before.

It looked like grain, and it was all over the bushes and everywhere.

It looked like a small, round seed of some kind.

"What is it? What is it?" everyone asked.

Moses said, "This is the bread that God promised to send to you from heaven."

And because the Israelite way of saying "What is it?" is "Man-hu?" the people gave the name "manna" to the food.

"You must gather the manna before the sun gets hot, Moses said.
"This means that you must gather it early.
"It will melt when the sun shines on it."

And the people noticed that this was true.
All that was left after the children of Israel had gathered what they needed disappeared when the sun got hot.

"You are to measure out two quarts for each person in your family," instructed Moses.

When the manna was measured, it always measured out to be exactly enough for everyone in the family.

This happened no matter how little or how much had been gathered.

Moses told the people to gather only as much as they needed for each day.

They were told not to try to gather enough for more than one day.

It would not be fit to eat if it was left over.

All the people were delighted with the taste of this food.

And they could make it into different things to eat.

They could boil the grain like meal for breakfast cereal.

They ground it into flour and made wafers and bread.

But however they fixed it, it tasted like something made with oil and honey.

Some of the people did not follow Moses' instructions about gathering the manna.

They thought it would be easier and save time if they gathered enough manna for several days.

And so they did.

But when they opened the jars of manna the next day—what a smell!

The manna had spoiled, and worms were

crawling all through it and it stank.

So that day the families of those who didn't follow instructions went hungry.

By the time those families discovered the rotten manna from the day before, it was too late to gather any manna for that day.

When Moses heard about it, he was very disgusted with those who had been too lazy to get up and gather the manna needed for the day.

But before the morning of the sixth day came, Moses gave the people some instructions about how much manna should be gathered on the morning of the sixth day.

Moses told the people that God was going to prove them by how well they obeyed His rules for gathering the manna.

"I will find out whether the people will obey My law or not," God had told Moses.

"On the sixth day," said Moses, "you are to gather twice as much as you gather on other days."

The gathering of the manna on the sixth day (Friday) was to be different.

The people were to gather a different amount.

So on the morning of the sixth day Moses reminded the people of what God had said.

Moses said to the people, "Tomorrow is the

holy Sabbath of the Lord.

"You will find no manna to gather in the morning.

"You are to do your baking and your boiling today.

"Eat what you need to eat for today.

"That which is left over you will put away for the Sabbath.

"It will keep.

"On the Sabbath you will eat what you have prepared on the sixth day.

"Six days the manna is to be gathered.

"On the sixth day you will gather twice as much as you gather on the other days.

"On the Sabbath day no manna will fall from heaven.

"The seventh day of the week is the Sabbath."

Most of the people did as the Lord had said.

But there were some who failed to obey.

These people went out on the Sabbath to gather manna as they did each day.

They discovered that there was not one bit of manna to gather.

Then God said to Moses, "How long are these people going to refuse to keep My commandments?

"I have given them My Sabbath.

"Bread for two days I give them on the sixth day.

"But no bread on the Sabbath."

When Moses told them what God said to him, the people listened.

God was trying to teach His people, who had forgotten about the holy Sabbath.

In this way He showed to them which day of the week is the Sabbath.

And all the people rested on the Sabbath day.

God gave the people the manna for forty long years.

Think of it—for forty years He showed them which day was the Sabbath.

Adam kept the Sabbath.

The ten patriarchs kept the Sabbath.

Enoch, Noah, and Abraham all knew which day was the Sabbath and kept the day holy.

When the Israelites first when down to Egypt, Jacob and his family must have been very particular about that day.

Of course, Joseph honored the day too.

But when the children of Israel were made slaves, they had a certain number of bricks to make each week.

They had so many bricks to make that it seemed to some of them that they would have to work on the Sabbath too.

In this way many of the people had failed to remember about this holy day.

Now God wanted to lead them back to a remembering of the Sabbath.

Now here in the wilderness God taught them about the Sabbath in a way they couldn't forget.

So the people rested on the Sabbath.

This means that they did not travel on that day.

But did it mean that they didn't do anything at all—did they sit in their tents all that day and do nothing?

No, there were things to do.

The animals had to be taken care of each day.

The cows had to be fed, watered, and milked.

The people didn't need to do much cooking because on the day before, they were to prepare the food that would be eaten on Sabbath.

They were to spend the Sabbath day thinking and talking about how God had been with them.

Think of all the stories that they knew.

The story about Adam and Eve in the beautiful garden.

The story of Noah and the Flood.

The wonderful stories of Abraham, Isaac, and Jacob.

They must never have tired of hearing about Joseph.

All had seen the wagon which carried Joseph's bones.

"Where are his bones going to be buried?" they must have asked.

They must have been curious about this.

"We'll bury them in the Promised Land," answered the fathers.

"That promise was made to Joseph before he died."

There are many things to discover and watch in the desert.

There were good times to be had in the desert if one didn't have to walk to keep up with his company.

The leaders were always calling, "Come on; come on; don't waste time.

"We must keep moving."

But on Sabbath everyone could really look around and not be hurried.

And to think the One who made all these things was the One who was in the cloud.

The One who was their Leader.

After a while the cloud lifted again.

It was time for the Israelites to move on.

They got their herds and flocks together.

Then the cloud led the Israelites out of the Wilderness of Sin.

Finally they stopped at a place called Rephidim.

They made camp there.

But they found no water.

God meant to test them again.

Water From the Rock

Now after their experiences in God's care, wouldn't you think the children of Israel would trust Him for a drink of water?

But they didn't.

They started grumbling again.

They were thirsty, very thirsty, after the tiresome march.

And now they found themselves in a place with no water.

The cloud had led them there.

So again the people came to Moses.

They demanded that he give them water.

Though they had yelled at Moses in anger, he answered them kindly.

"Why do you blame me?" asked Moses.

"God is the One who is leading us.
"Why do you try God's patience?"

"Moses doesn't know what he is doing.
"Why did we ever follow him out of Egypt?" shouted the angry mob.
"Have you brought us out here to kill us and our children and our cattle with thirst?" they screamed.

How rude they were to Moses!
They acted as if they hated him.
They started to pick up stones to throw at him.

Moses asked them to be quiet.
But they were all so angry and beside themselves in rage that no one could be heard.
Can you imagine Moses standing there, very still, praying?

"What can I do with these people?
"They are almost ready to stone me."

"Take your rod and call all the elders of the tribes together," the Lord answered Moses.
"You are to take the elders with you and go up to the big rock on Mount Horeb.
"I will meet you there.
"I will stand beside you there, though the people will not see me.
"But I will stand on the rock beside you.

"You will strike the rock with your rod.
"I will cause water to come out of the rock."

Moses did just what the Lord said to do.
He took his rod.
Then he called the elders of each tribe to come with him to the mountain.
The elders followed as Moses led the way to the big rock on Mount Horeb.
And there, while the elders watched, Moses struck the rock with his rod.
Out gushed the wonderful water down the mountainside, and on it flowed into the camp of the Israelites.
Yes, everyone had all the water he needed.

"God was with us there on the rock," Moses told the elders.
"It was he who made the water flow when I struck it with my rod.
"It wasn't what I did that gave the water to us."

We can be sure that all in the whole camp heard about how God gave them water when they were so thirsty.

How God Destroyed the Amalekites

The children of Israel had come quite a distance from Egypt.

God had led them all the way.

But now a new danger threatened.

The Amalekites, a very wicked, cruel people, lived near Mount Sinai.

The Amalekites were descendants of Amalek, a grandson of Esau.

Esau had been Jacob's twin brother.

Esau had not wanted to serve the God of his father, Jacob.

He hadn't cared about the birthright.

The Amalekites were descendants of Esau.

These descendants of Esau knew about the true God.

Instead of serving and fearing the true God,

they set themselves to defy His power.

The Amalekites had heard of the wonders that God had worked in Egypt.

And they had made fun of the Egyptians because of this.

Because the surrounding nations were afraid to attack the Israelites, the Amalekites made fun of them.

These wicked Amalekites had boasted that they would destroy God's people.

They even took an oath by their gods that they would not allow one of the children of Israel to escape.

"Israel's God will be powerless to resist us," these wicked people bragged.

"We will attack them and destroy them, and by so doing we will show that we hate and defy God."

And so they boasted and so they planned.
The Amalekites had long been very wicked.
Yet God had still called them to repent.
God wants everyone to obey Him and be happy.
Satan and his evil angels were now urging the Amalekites to destroy God's own people.

As they listened to and followed Satan's urging, these wicked people lost their last chance to repent.

When Moses learned what the Amalekites were planning, he thought and prayed about what could be done.

The Israelites had done nothing to provoke or hurt the Amalekites, but the Amalekites had attacked the Israelites.

Moses chose Joshua (one of the leaders) to select a body of soldiers from the different tribes to defend the Israelites.

Joshua was to lead these soldiers the next day against the enemy.

Moses would stand on a high hill nearby with the rod of God in his hand.

According to the plan, Joshua and his company would attack the enemy.

Moses and Aaron and Hur went to the hill which overlooked the battlefield.

With his arms outstretched to heaven, and holding his rod in his hand, Moses prayed.

Moses prayed that God would help the army of Israel.

Aaron and Hur saw that as long as Moses' hands were reaching upward, God's people were winning the battle.

But when his hands got heavy and he couldn't keep them up, the Amalekites seemed to win.

So Aaron and Hur held up Moses' hands.

Moses sat on a big rock and prayed.

Aaron stood on one side of Moses.

Hur stood on the other side of Moses.

Moses held the rod in his hand.

Moses, with Aaron and Hur, stayed on the hill until the sun went down.

The Amalekites lost the battle and ran away.

Satan had lost again.

The surrounding nations learned that the bragging, wicked nation of the Amalekites had been defeated by the God of Israel.

They had learned more about the power of the great God of the Israelites.

After the defeat of the Amalekites, God told Moses, "I want you to write about this day in a book and tell it to Joshua, for I will blot out the remembrance of Amalek from under heaven."

Moses' Family Joins Him

One day Moses received some very happy news.

The whole camp of Israel was pitched not far from the home of Moses' father-in-law, Jethro.

Moses' wife, Zipporah, and his two sons had been staying with Jethro while Moses was away.

Now Jethro decided they should all go and see Moses.

It had been almost a year since Moses had left Midian and gone back to Egypt.

The two boys, Gershom and Eliezer, were excited to think that they were going to see their father again.

They could hardly wait to get there.

Someone told Moses that his family and Jethro were coming.

He went out to meet them.

What joy it was to see each other again!

Moses had sent his family back to Midian when he went to Egypt, because he had feared for their safety in Egypt.

But now how happy they all were to be together again.

Not only was Moses delighted to see Zipporah and his two sons, but he was also glad that Jethro was there.

Moses took them all to his tent.

Then Moses told of the wonderful way in which God had led the people and cared for them.

They listened to the story of the Red Sea, about the water being made sweet, about the quail and the manna, and the water from the rock, and the Amalekites.

Jethro was happy to hear how God had blessed the children of Israel.

And Jethro said to Moses, "Blessed be the Lord, who has delivered you out of the hand of the Egyptians.

"Now I know that the Lord is greater than all other gods."

Then Jethro, Moses' father-in-law, presented a burnt offering and sacrifices for God.

And Aaron and all the elders of Israel came to eat bread with Moses' father-in-law before God.

They had a great feast.

Jethro stayed with Moses for some time.

Moses was glad to

have his father-in-law, his wife, and sons with him again.

Jethro was a very kind and wise man.

He watched what was going on in camp.

He saw how the people came to Moses with all their problems.

Zipporah had talked to her father, telling him she felt concern for Moses' health.

"He is being worn out by all the things he has to take care of with these people," she said.

"I can tell that he is very weary.

"Maybe you can help him," Zipporah suggested.

And as Jethro watched the people and listened to what they said, he tried to think how he could help Moses.

When Jethro talked with Moses about the problem, Moses tried to explain about it.

"I have encouraged the people to come to me," said Moses.

"It gives me a chance to help them.

"I help them to know about God's statutes and His laws."

"But," said Jethro, "it is too much for you.

"You are not able to do it all by yourself alone.

"You are working too hard.

"You will wear yourself out."

Then Jethro suggested a plan to help Moses.

"Choose some good, able men who fear God.

"These should be men of truth, men who hate wanting other people's things.

"Let some of these men be rulers of thousands, others be rulers of hundreds, and others be rulers of tens.

"Let these men judge in small matters.

"The important matters will be for you to take care of, Moses.

"So you will teach the people about the laws of God and how they should walk before God.

"They will also learn about the work that they should do."

Moses accepted Jethro's plan.

Not only did the plan help Moses, but it also helped to keep better order in the camp.

The time came when Jethro had to return to his home in Midian.

Moses' family stayed with him and the camp of Israel.

As Jethro parted from those he loved, he was sad.

But he could always remember that he had been able to help with the work of the great camp of God's people.

From Rephidim the people continued on their journey as they followed the cloud.

The cloud led them across barren plains, through pleasant valleys, and up over steep places.

Sometimes they saw before them such high mountains that they wondered how they would get over them.

But the cloud led and they followed, and always they found openings between these mountains to let them through.

Then beyond the passes they would see other plains, then mountains again.

And now, through the last of the passes the children of Israel were led.

On both sides of the pass were rocky cliffs rising hundreds of feet high.

Between those high rocky cliffs marched the children of Israel with their flocks and herds.

As far as one could see, the great caravan traveled on with the cloud.

As they came through this last pass the people caught the sight of Mount Sinai.

At the top of Mount Sinai the cloud rested.

The people spread their tents on the plain.

Here was to be their home for nearly a year.

God had told Moses at the burning bush that he and God's people would worship at this mountain.

And here they were, just as God had said.

God had led them all the way from slavery to this place.

But He had promised to take them to the Land of Canaan.

Would He keep that promise?

Sinai at Last

For three months the children of Israel had been traveling.

They had traveled through the Red Sea and through the wilderness.

God had protected them from the hot sun.

He had given them manna from heaven to eat.

He had given them water from the rock to drink.

He had destroyed their enemies the Amalekites.

God had led them and cared for them every step of the way from Egypt to Sinai.

Now they pitched their camp at the foot of the mountain.

The pillar of cloud rested there on Sinai; so the children of Israel knew this was a stopping place.

Now God called to Moses to come up into the mountain.

He wanted to talk to him.

This is the message God gave Moses to deliver to the people:

"You have seen what I did unto the Egyptians and how I have cared for you.

"Now, if you will obey Me and keep My covenant, then you will be a special treasure unto Me above all people, for all the earth is Mine."

When Moses went back to the camp and called the people together, he gave them God's message.

They listened to Moses' words.

The people quickly promised that all that the Lord said, they would do.

Moses went back up the mountain slope and told the Lord that the people had agreed to keep their end of the promise.

God told Moses that He had come in a thick cloud on the mount so that the people would hear Him speak.

Then they would know that Moses was God's chosen leader.

When the people had met with difficulties along the way, they had complained that Moses had led them from Egypt to destroy them.

Now the Lord honored Moses so the people would believe in him and have confidence in his leading.

Once more the Lord sent Moses back down the mountain to the people.

The Lord told Moses that the people were now to make special preparation to hear Him speak to them.

The Lord planned to give the children of Israel His law.

But first of all they must realize the exalted character of God.

The Lord told Moses to have the people get rid of all their sins by confessing and repenting.

They were then to cleanse their bodies by bathing.

They were to have clean clothes to put on.

Moses was instructed to build a fence or barrier at the base of the mountain.

He was to tell the people that no one—no person or animal—should go beyond the fence.

The mountain, Mount Sinai, where the Lord would appear in all his splendor and glory, was holy ground.

On the morning of the third day the people were ready.

They gathered at the foot of the mountain.

They looked with solemn eyes at the thick, black cloud that covered the mountain.

Lightning began to flash from the cloud, and thunder rolled and echoed and reechoed among the surrounding mountaintops.

The people heard the sound of a trumpet.

The sound grew louder and louder.

The people trembled.

Then suddenly the thunder stopped.

The trumpet sound stopped.
Everything was silent.
Then the Lord spoke.
The people standing at the foot of the mountain listened.

"I am the Lord thy God, which have brought thee out of the land of Egypt, out of the house of bondage."

Now that the children of Israel were free from slavery, God wanted them to be the keepers of His law.

He expected them, the people whom He had so miraculously delivered, to show to the heathen nations around them the true character of the God who had created the earth and all that was in it.

Here at Mount Sinai God spoke His law so all the people could hear.

Later He would give them the commandments written on tables of stone, but He wanted the people to have His law not only on the tables of stone, but also in their hearts.

God wanted them to keep His commandments not just because they were law, but because the people loved the Lawgiver and wanted to do the things that He wanted them to do.

Surely this God was a God they could love and trust.

He had led them from their days of slavery in Egypt.

He had led them through the Red Sea.

He had destroyed their enemies who would have destroyed them.

He had given them food from heaven and fresh water from a rock.

He had shielded them from the burning rays of the sun in the desert.

This was the God who had led them out of the land of Egypt to Sinai.

This was the God who now spoke to them, giving them the law.

The law would make them a happy nation, and the other nations would see that the children of Israel were different.

The other nations would want to be like them.

The children of Israel stood at the foot of the mountain and listened to the voice of God coming from the cloud on top of the mountain.

They heard Him say, "I am the Lord thy God,

which have brought thee out of the land of Egypt, out of the house of bondage."

And then the Lord spoke the commandments.

When He had finished speaking, the people were afraid.

God now gave Moses certain civil laws that the people should obey.

When Moses told the people these laws, they all said, "All the words which the Lord hath said will we do."

Then the Lord called Moses up into the mountain again.

Moses was not the only one that God called to come up into the mountain.

He also called Joshua to come up with Moses.

Moses and Joshua went up the mountain together.

Moses was told to come into the cloud, into the presence of God.

Joshua was told to wait for Moses.

While Moses and God were together in the cloud, the children of Israel, who were waiting at the foot of the mountain should have been praying and thinking of the things that God had said to them.

They wondered what was going on in the Mount.

While Moses was in the cloud with God, God gave him the ten commandments written on two tables of stone.

The Ten Commandments

1

Thou shalt have no other gods before me.

2

Thou shalt not make unto thee any graven image, or any likeness of any thing that is in heaven above, or that is in the earth beneath, or that is in the water under the earth: thou shalt not bow down thyself to them, nor serve them: for I the Lord thy God am a jealous God, visiting the iniquity of the fathers upon the children unto the third and fourth generation of them that hate me; and shewing mercy unto thousands of them that love me, and keep my commandments.

3

Thou shalt not take the name of the Lord thy God in vain; for the Lord will not hold him guiltless that taketh his name in vain.

4

Remember the sabbath day, to keep it holy. Six days shalt thou labour, and do all thy work: but the seventh day is the sabbath of the Lord thy God: in it thou shalt not do any work, thou, nor thy son, nor thy daughter, thy manservant, nor thy maidservant, nor thy cattle, nor thy stranger that is within thy gates: for in six days the Lord made heaven and earth, the sea, and all that in them is, and rested the seventh day: wherefore the Lord blessed the sabbath day, and hallowed it.

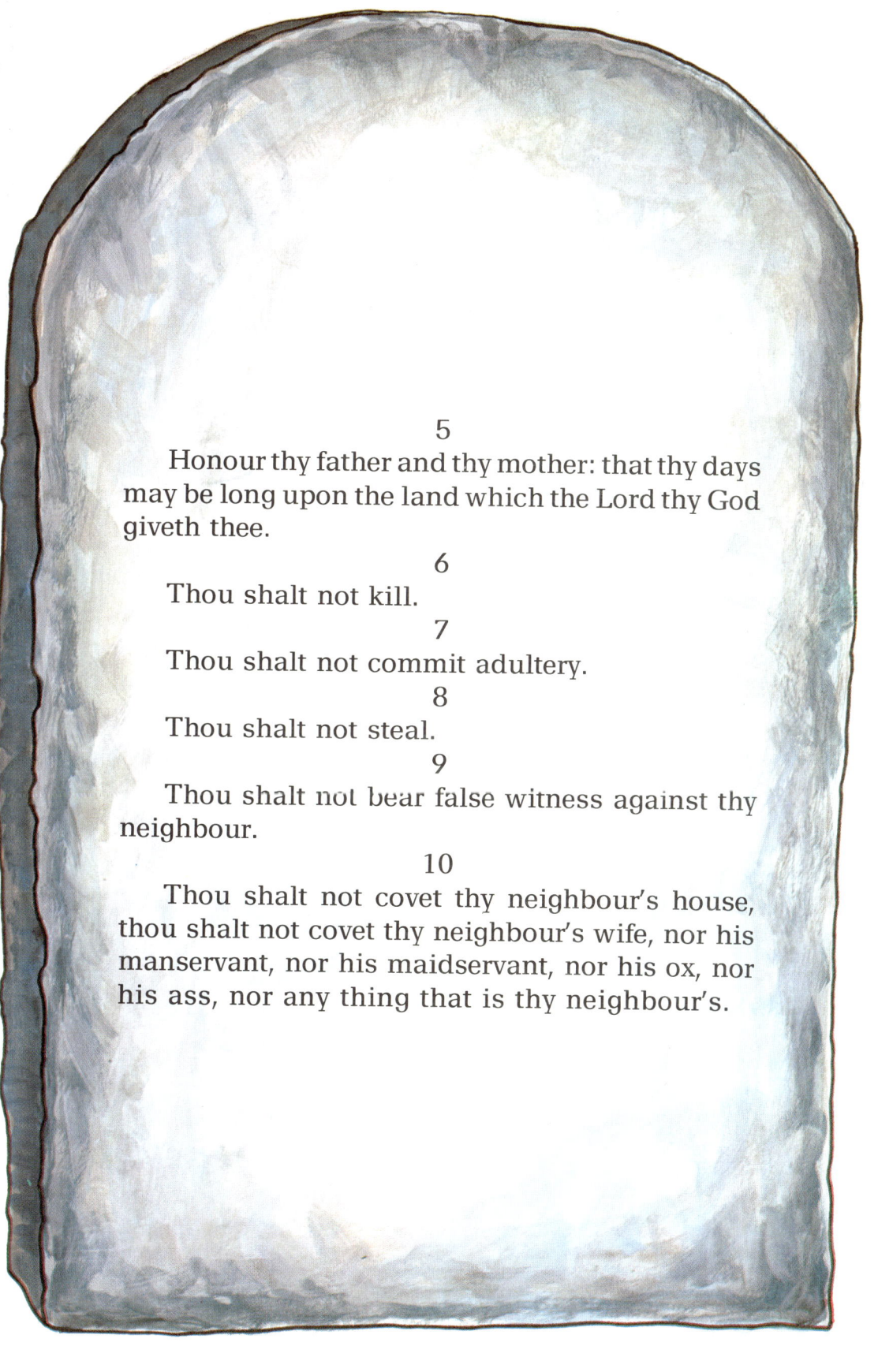

5

Honour thy father and thy mother: that thy days may be long upon the land which the Lord thy God giveth thee.

6

Thou shalt not kill.

7

Thou shalt not commit adultery.

8

Thou shalt not steal.

9

Thou shalt not bear false witness against thy neighbour.

10

Thou shalt not covet thy neighbour's house, thou shalt not covet thy neighbour's wife, nor his manservant, nor his maidservant, nor his ox, nor his ass, nor any thing that is thy neighbour's.

The children of Israel wondered what had happened to Moses up there in the cloud on the mountain—he had been gone so long.

Perhaps he would never return.

They began to think of the land of Egypt, and they remembered the gods of Egypt.

They soon came to Aaron who had been left to care for the camp, and asked him to make them a god.

Aaron was afraid the people would kill him if he didn't do as they asked.

From the gold and silver they brought to him, he made a golden calf—just like the ones worshiped in Egypt.

The people had forgotten their promise to obey God and have no other gods before Him.

They began to shout and dance and sing and worship the golden calf.

God knew what the people were doing.

He told Moses to hurry down to the people.

Since they had not kept their promise to God, He said He would destroy them.

But Moses begged God to forgive them.

Moses was willing to be destroyed himself if God would only forgive the people.

Moses and Joshua hurried down to the camp.

When Moses saw what the people were doing, he became so angry, and yet sad, that he threw down the tables of stone and they were broken in pieces.

Could God ever really forgive these people?